¿Cómo crece? / How Does It Grow?

# ¿CÓMO CRECE EL PASTO?
# HOW DOES GRASS GROW?

Kathleen Connors
Traducido por / Translated by Diana Osorio

Please visit our website, www.garethstevens.com. For a free color catalog of all our high-quality books, call toll free 1-800-542-2595 or fax 1-877-542-2596.

Library of Congress Cataloging-in-Publication Data
Names: Connors, Kathleen, author.
Title: ¿Cómo creceel pasto? / How Does Grass Grow? / Kathleen Connors.
Description: New York : Gareth Stevens Publishing, [2022] | Series: ¿Cómo
   Crece? / How Does It Grow? | Includes index.
Identifiers: LCCN 2020012337 | ISBN 9781538269473 (library binding) | ISBN 9781538269480
   (ebook)
Subjects: LCSH: Grasses–Juvenile literature.
Classification: LCC SB197 .C65 2022 | DDC 633.2–dc23
LC record available at https://lccn.loc.gov/2020012337

First Edition

Published in 2022 by
**Gareth Stevens Publishing**
111 East 14th Street, Suite 349
New York, NY 10003

Copyright © 2022 Gareth Stevens Publishing

Translator: Diana Osorio
Editor, Spanish: Rossana Zúñiga
Editor, English: Kristen Nelson
Designer: Katelyn E. Reynolds

Photo credits: Cover, p.1 Tim Hawley / Photographer's Choice / Getty Images Plus; p. 5 Ning Li/Moment/ Getty Images; pp. 7, 24 (seeds) georgeclerk/E+/Getty Images; pp. 9, 24 (soil) Faba-Photograhpy/Moment/ Getty Images; p. 11 oxign/E+/Getty Images; pp. 13, 24 (roots) redmal/E+/Getty Images; p. 15 VR19/ iStock/ Getty Images Plus; p. 17 Jacky Parker Photography/Moment/Getty Images; p. 19 Mint Images RF/Getty Images; p. 21 Sheryl Watson/ iStock / Getty Images Plus; p. 23 WILLIAM WEST/AFP via Getty Images.

All rights reserved. No part of this book may be reproduced in any form without permission in writing from the publisher, except by a reviewer.

Printed in the United States of America

Some of the images in this book illustrate individuals who are models. The depictions do not imply actual situations or events.

CPSIA compliance information: Batch #CSGS22: For further information contact Gareth Stevens, New York, New York at 1-800-542-2595.

# Contenido

El crecimiento del pasto . . . . . . . . . . . . . . 4

Lo que necesita el pasto . . . . . . . . . . . . . 8

Un campo de pasto . . . . . . . . . . . . . . 12

Alimento para animales . . . . . . . . . . . . 22

Palabras que debes aprender . . . . . . . . . 24

Índice . . . . . . . . . . . . . . . . . . . . . . 24

# Contents

Growing Grass . . . . . . . . . . . . . . . . . 4

What Grass Needs. . . . . . . . . . . . . . . . 8

Field of Grasses . . . . . . . . . . . . . . . 12

Animal Food . . . . . . . . . . . . . . . . . 22

Words to Know . . . . . . . . . . . . . . . . 24

Index. . . . . . . . . . . . . . . . . . . . . . 24

¡El pasto está en nuestro alrededor!
¿Cómo crece?

..............................................

Grass is all around us!
How does it grow?

El pasto crece
de las semillas.
¡Las semillas son pequeñas!

..............................

Grass grows from seeds.
The seeds are tiny!

7

Crece en la tierra.

· · · · · · · · · · · · · · · · · · · · · · · · · ·

They grow in soil.

Necesita agua.
También necesita
la luz del sol.

. . . . . . . . . . . . . . . . . . . . . . . . . . . . . .

They need water.
They need sunlight too.

Las semillas brotan.
Crecen hojas y raíces.

. . . . . . . . . . . . . . . . . . . . . . . . . . . . . . . . .

The seeds sprout.
Leaves and roots grow.

Esto puede demorar
alrededor de
dos semanas.

........................................

This can take about
two weeks.

15

Hay muchos tipos
de pasto.

......................................

There are many kinds
of grass.

El trigo es un pasto.
¡Podemos comerlo!

..................................

Wheat is a grass.
People can eat it!

El lolium es verde.
¡Puede crecer en tu jardín!

. . . . . . . . . . . . . . . . . . . . . . . . . . . . . . .

Ryegrass is green.
It may grow in your yard!

Las vacas comen pasto.
También les ayuda
a crecer.

..............................

Cows eat grass.
It helps them grow too.

23

# Palabras que debes aprender
# Words to Know

raíces/
roots

semillas/
seeds

tierra/
soil

## Índice / Index

hojas / leaves, 12

lolium / ryegrass, 20

trigo / wheat, 18

24